FACT IS:

TRUTH IS

FACT IS:

TRUTH IS

DR. FREDDY B. WILSON

Introduction

Internationally people are always seeking the truth. Some people will probably say that truth and fact are one in the same. I venture to say they are not the same. There is a popular line in a film that says, "You can't handle the truth!" And then there are facts. Facts could be defined as things that are unchangeable and are solid. There is a popular line in an old television program that asks for, "Just the facts, ma'am". Truth can depend on how people view certain things or legal precedence or belief system. Information found here will show how truth can go beyond the facts in any given situation.

There are varying definitions of the word "fact" found on the Internet:

- A piece of information about circumstances that exist or events that have occurred; "first you must collect all the facts of the case"

- A statement or assertion of verified information about something that is the case or has happened; "he supported his argument with an impressive array of facts"

- An event known to have happened or something known to have existed; "your fears have no basis in fact"; "how much of the story is fact and how much fiction is hard to tell"

- A concept whose truth can be proved; "scientific hypotheses are not facts" (wordnet.princeton.edu/perl/webwn)

- Something that is known to have happened or to be true or to exist (resweb.llu.edu/rford/docs/VGD/GSLVT/gs lglossary.html)

- A detail that can be measured or researched. Mathematical principles are based on facts. (www.arlington.k12.va.us/gunston/gen_inf o/sols/index.html)

- A truth based on accurate information or thing known to have occurred (myths.e2bn.net/mythsandlegends/view_glo ssary_16_F.html)

There are also varying definitions of the word "truth" found on the Internet:

- A fact that has been verified; "at last he knew the truth"; "the truth is that he didn't want to do it".

- Conformity to reality or actuality; "they debated the truth of the proposition"; "the situation brought home to us the blunt truth of the military threat"; "he was famous for the truth of his portraits"; "he turned to religion in his search for eternal verities".

- A true statement; "he told the truth"; "he thought of answering with the truth but he knew they wouldn't believe it".

- Accuracy: the quality of being near to the true value; "he was beginning to doubt the accuracy of his compass"; "the lawyer questioned the truth of my account". (wordnet.princeton.edu/perl/webwn)

Phil Ryan said, "There are puzzles in the way we speak of truth, and it is prudent not to sweep these aside through a restrictive definition." (Ryan, 2005) This means that if we get lost in restricting the definition of truth, it would be hard to believe it when something happens that does not fit the norm. I believe while living your life for God many things will happen to you that could not be simply defined by scientific terms. We live in the natural world while God works his blessings in the supernatural.

H. Kent Craig said, "The difference between "the truth" and "the facts" is not philosophical hair-splitting; it's actually quite orthodox. While something is either true or not, and something is a fact or not, something can be a fact without being true and can be true without being a fact." (Craig,

2006) You can be going through something in your life that is a fact and a solution may seem impossible. The truth is that God can bless you to overcome your situation miraculously. The results of which could not be duplicated. Craig gives us a different contrast between the two in an example by saying, "It is true that you get paid every pay period. But is it a fact that you'll be paid on time next one?" (Craig, 2006)

Sometimes what we see as fact does not always prove to be true. "The best "fact" in the world is one that is so manifest that its existence can simply not be disputed." (Craig, 2006) We often live by and believe in only what we can see. As believers in God, we cannot always go by and depend on what we see. Let's not be complex here. We must acknowledge what we see to actually exist but through faith and belief we must also know that God can change any given situation or circumstance. In other words, God can change the facts in our lives through the truth in his Word. Matthew McGrath said, "Lynch would not argue that the value of truth is to be found in, say, the fact that it distributes across conjunction while falsity does not." (McGrath, 2005)

McGrath states, "Lynch might reply that this is no problem: 'I *do* have an explanation of why it's good to believe the truth, even if it doesn't involve any assumption about the nature of truth. It's good to believe the truth because of its part in self-respect, integrity, sincerity, and ultimately happiness.'" (McGrath, 2005) The Bible teaches us that believing in truth is a part of faith. Having the faith to believe in the truth will not always come easily. Many scholars have tackled the ideas behind truth for many years but tried to base it on science. Scientific facts have changed over years but the truth has not!

McGrath said, "General facts may be grounded collectively by their instances. And so, if the instances of a general fact about truth are grounded, then the general fact itself is grounded, and in that sense explained." (McGrath, 2005) Allow me to take this a little further. Richard L. Gorsuch said, "Although seldom developed philosophically, science accepts a finding as a fact if and only if another experimenter replicates it." (Gorsuch, 2002)

Gorsuch went on to say, "In the perspective of falsifiability and replication, it is difficult for religion—as well as for the rest of the humanities—to be considered a truth issue because most religious statements are nonfalsifiable and important aspects of religion—such as revelation—cannot be replicated." Gorsuch was only referring to a worldly view of what others consider to be the truth. We should not base the truth on mere 'religion'. Our relationships with God will prevail to us a truth that man cannot easily define.

T. Lee Burnham, University of Phoenix, said, "The ancient Greeks believed that truth was obtainable. Socrates put his trust in appropriate question asking and introspection. Plato distrusted perception and relied on pure logic. In the Medieval World truth was available from God. In the beginnings of the Modern World science and scientific law was seen as the source of truth." (Burnham, 2003)

To put this in further perspective, Miriam defined truth as "a Primary Principle, means conformity with fact, agreement with reality, accuracy, correctness, verity of a statement or thought, genuineness, reality, conduct following the divine standard, spirituality of life and behavior, that which is true, real, or actual in a general or abstract sense ..." (miriams-well.org/Glossary/index.html). As observed from this definition, truth is not something easily identified by earthly standards. You have to grow in your relationship with God to find any real truths in life. Even then you may not understand the truth in what God is showing you or is trying to do for you.

This is where you have to distinguish between truths and facts. Gorsuch said, "A fact is established when people running the same research study get the same results. Fact is not from some magical way to truth of a radically different nature from what is believed to be the truth of everyday life. Fact is instead based on a data consistency, that is, an outcome that occurs when data are collected under the standardized conditions of the experiment. Scientific *fact* is quite distinct from scientific *theory* (although the two interact)". (Gorsuch, 2002)

"There are cases of attempted replication that have not yet worked. A prime example is that of cold fusion (Friedlander, 1995). Fusion had occurred previously in theory and in reports of it but only at very high temperatures, such as inside of a star. So when the scientists thought they had observed fusion at room temperatures, they were excited and introduced their experiment in a news conference.

The cold-fusion experiment was "low-tech" and easily replicated. Many scientists had the necessary equipment in their laboratories to try the experiment. And many did, but they did not find the same results. Because the results have not yet been generally replicated, cold fusion has not been accepted as a scientific fact.

There were other factors involved in scientists' reactions to cold fusion (Friedlander, 1995). Scientists challenged the study because they doubted what had happened. These doubts were because the results contradicted other facts, as scientists

7

understood them, about fusion and the theory of fusion. The press reported these doubts often. For science, the rejection was neither because of past research nor because of current theory but was because the other scientists could not replicate the results. Rejection of an experiment may be in part because it violates past research or current theory, but the prime essential is replication." (Gorsuch, 2002)

Science is fundamentally needed in the world for man to progress. Conversely, we must not put all our beliefs in science. For science, truth is defined by being able to repeat a certain act or event. In Christian life God will enable us to do things where He will perform miracles that cannot be repeated or understood by man.

Gorsuch said, "First, the Judeo-Christian-Islamic theology noted that "God is the same yesterday, today, and tomorrow" (Heb. 13:8). This provided a worldview that expects to find a universe that "is the same yesterday, today, and tomorrow." The universe has basic characteristics that are the same from one day to the next. Without such a worldview, science is not reasonable. We would have no basis to check for replicable facts.

A second major theological point supporting the development of classical science is the role of people in relationship to the world. The Bible is clear that we are given dominion over the world (Gen. 1:28). That is illustrated in Genesis when God brings all the creatures to be named by people. It means that although we do not have ownership, we do have control and responsibility for how we use that control. Control means that we can change things, and that is a necessary assumption for the experiment to be a basis for understanding reality. Because we have dominion over the world, we also need to know that world in depth to make right decisions in carrying out the responsibility that goes with that dominion." (Gorsuch, 2002)

God has blessed man on earth to understand how things work through studies in science. There are many disciplines in science and there are many religions throughout the world. The God-based religions believe in the ultimate and inexplicable power of God. Gorsuch said, "The disciplines that are most linked to the idiographic events of life are in the arts and humanities, including religion. They express our situations, including spiritual ones, in ways that communicate in matters that go beyond the replicable exposition of nomothetic science." (Gorsuch, 2002)

Gorsuch went on to say, "Religion is part of the humanities. Its primary concern is with unique, idiographic events. Consider Christianity. It considers God to have been revealed in historical events, such as bringing the Hebrews out of slavery and the crucifixion of Jesus. Because these are unique events with no possibility of being studied by the nomothetic methods of science, they can only be studied by methods of humanities, such as history, concerned with unique, nonreplicable events." (Gorsuch, 2002) The truth in the changes in your life cannot be replicated by man. No matter what you are told or what you see with your eyes, keep the faith in God to know His truth will always prevail!

I think a relationship with God goes beyond mere 'religion'. We must put our efforts into our relationship with God. There is too much focus in society for those that believe in God on their various religions or specific Christian denominations. In the Christian community, I assert that no one denomination is getting into Heaven any faster or more assured than another. There are many people who participate in what could be called "organized religion" who do not have personal relationships with God. These people are often the most notable people in the organization or congregation. Unfortunately, when these people get into their worldly trouble, it makes the whole religious organization or church look bad. The outside public rarely takes the time to associate the problem solely with the individual. None are us are perfect and we are in constant need of prayer. We should strive to be consistently Christ-like in both our public and private lives. Don't pretend to be a perfect Christian when you're at church or around Church members, then be the biggest devil and liar when you're around close friends and family!

"As the illustration of prayer shows, there is a basic problem in scientific investigation of God's individual activities in the world. Science can and does, from a Christian view, identify how God continually and steadfastly operates time after time. These acts of God are replicable, because they occur consistently time after time. The problem with investigating God's individual acts, such as in prayer research, is that the act is for an individual, idiographic event. Christianity holds that God operates at an idiographic, individual level and at the level of nomothetic law. We call the former actions "miracles" if they are spectacular and seen through the eye of faith. But they cannot be confirmed or refuted by science, being at the idiographic level. Why can science neither confirm nor refute an individual act of God?

Because the heart of science's method is replication. If it replicates, then a scientific conclusion can be drawn. If it does not replicate, then no scientific conclusion can be drawn. By *definition*, God's individual acts do not replicate. So science can never identify them even if they happen a dozen times a day

11

in every scientist's life." (Gorsuch, 2002) Don't become that "educated fool" who becomes so educated that no one can tell you about God's power because it has not been proven by scientists or people in your educated social circles. Seek God in all you do and He will reveal himself to you.

"The emphasis on personal experience in science has been long known. "One of the hallmarks of James' philosophy is its insistence on experience as the ultimate point of justification for any proposed truth" (Vanden Burgt, 1981, p. 56). James (1904/1985) is clear as to "how reality is established. It comes to us in personal experiences based on direct experiences" (Gorsuch & Spilka, 1987, p. 775)." (Gorsuch, 2002)

Differences Between Fact and Truth

The differences between Fact and Truth is that fact is the "what" you are going through and the truth is that the problems you experience have some ultimate purpose. The truth is the problems are designed to prepare you for something greater. Going through problems is never easy. However, it is often necessary. The lessons learned when going through problems helps develop our character and builds our faith. Exalt God for just being God even when things don't seem to be going your way.

> **Acts 2:33 (NLT)** [33]Now he is exalted to the place of highest honor in heaven, at God's right hand. And the Father, as he had promised, gave him the Holy Spirit to pour out upon us, just as you see and hear today.

Our experiences in life are what make us the persons we have become. We shouldn't always demand that God shows us in advance how he is going to bless us. The truth is that the bigger your faith in God, the bigger your blessings will be.

"Because our personal experience contains that which we assume is true without further evidence

13

and because even science is ultimately based on personal experience, it is our unique, idiographic personal experiences that provide the best evidence for what we believe as truth." (Gorsuch, 2002)

> **Mark 2:9 - 12 (NLT)** [9]Is it easier to say to the paralyzed man 'Your sins are forgiven,' or 'Stand up, pick up your mat, and walk'? [10]So I will prove to you that the Son of Man has the authority on earth to forgive sins." Then Jesus turned to the paralyzed man and said, [11]"Stand up, pick up your mat, and go home!" [12]And the man jumped up, grabbed his mat, and walked out through the stunned onlookers. They were all amazed and praised God, exclaiming, "We've never seen anything like this before!"

We have to have faith in the things that we cannot see. God will bless us in so many ways that we previously thought were impossible. The fact is I only make a certain amount of money. The truth is regardless of how much money I make compared to someone else, God has blessed me far beyond the amount of money I make. The favor of God is real!

Just as He has done for me, God is capable of doing any and all things on your behalf.

> **Romans 4:17 (NLT)** [17]That is what the Scriptures mean when God told him, "I have made you the father of many nations." This happened because Abraham believed in the God who brings the dead back to life and who creates new things out of nothing.

You may ask how I apply all these truths to change the facts in my life. Let's begin by discussing how you can use the Word of the Lord to protect yourself. I have learned over the years about the pieces of armor Christians can use.

> **Mark 11:22 - 24 (NLT)** [22]Then Jesus said to the disciples, "Have faith in God. [23]I tell you the truth, you can say to this mountain, 'May you be lifted up and thrown into the sea,' and it will happen. But you must really believe it will happen and have no doubt in your heart. [24]I tell you, you can pray for anything,

> and if you believe that you've
> received it, it will be yours.

Remember, the truth is that the armor we use is not carnal, but spiritual.

-   We must use the helmet of salvation. We do this by watching what goes in our heads. We must be careful of the things we watch on TV, the type of movies we watch, the books we read, and what we listen to from other people.

-   We must use the breast plate of righteousness. What is right is found in the Bible. Reading it often will lead us further onto the path of righteousness.

-   We must wear the belt of honor. We do this by learning and living in truth. The Bible provides guidelines for us to follow.

-   We must chard our feet with the gospel of peace. There are many people who love to create disturbances in our lives. This can be seen both at work and in our homes. We must not let these disturbances distract us from the purpose God puts on our lives.

-   We must pray in the Spirit. There are many people that pray and don't really know where their prayers go. Some folk pray only because that is what they were taught and it does not go much further than that. Having a relationship with God and having full faith in Him takes prayer to a different level.

A fact is there are some difficult things that the people of God are experiencing in their everyday lives. A lot of it comes from their marriages. There are some games married people plays.

- One of the games is putting on masks. One or both of the marriage partners do this by acting like someone they really are not. An example would be one pretending to be a faithful Christian when privately they are one of the most devilish persons they could be.

- Another game is that of not being truthful. Some people find it easier to not tell the truth than face the negativity they perceive they would receive by telling the truth.

- There are problems if there is competition or power struggles between couples. This happens when one person feels they have to be just as capable or successful as their partner. This is especially prevalent in dual-income families. This competition or power struggle only brings about bitterness.

17

Our family structure has already been defined by God. Women should not feel they have to control their husbands and men should not feel they have to dominate their wives. Christians need to learn to walk in truth and love. Our truth is embedded in our faith in God. We must do right as defined by God's Word. This will provide us an excellent spirit. Having an excellent spirit will compel you to always try to do right, even when you don't feel like it. Remember the truth cannot transform you until you accept it!!

> **1 Corinthians 4:20 - 21 (NLT)**
> [20]For the Kingdom of God is not just a lot of talk; it is living by God's power. [21]Which do you choose? Should I come with a rod to punish you, or should I come with love and a gentle spirit?

Truth is choosing God's Word will provide us with unseen power. This power will aid us in defeating any attack from the devil. The most powerful weapon we have against the devil is love. We must continually show our family love even when they disappoint us. There may be many negative facts based on actions from our family. The truth is when you forgive and apply Godly principals to the problems, God can deliver us from any problems we face.

> **Philemon 1:3 - 7 (NLT)** [3]May God our Father and the Lord Jesus Christ give you grace and peace. [4]I always thank my God when I pray for you, Philemon, [5]because I keep hearing about your faith in the Lord Jesus and your love for all of God's people. [6]And I am praying that you will put into action the generosity that comes from your faith as you understand and experience all the good things we have in Christ. [7]Your love has given me much joy and comfort, my brother, for your kindness has often refreshed the hearts of God's people.

Michael Scott said, "A central challenge for a Christian theology of truth is to reach an understanding of the claim that Jesus is the truth. In John's Gospel, Jesus tells his disciples "I am the way, the truth, and the life" (14:6), and in 1 John truth is predicated of the Holy Spirit (5:6). Moreover, the seemingly unresolved discussion about truth between Jesus and Pilate might plausibly be interpreted as an example of Johannine irony: Pilate asks Jesus "What is truth?" ignorant of the fact that the answer is the person he is addressing." (Scott, 2005)

We must believe the truth about Jesus being the son of God. This goes beyond just believing in the stories we are told when we were young or the Bible stories we read. If you grew up in a family that believed in God, that only gave us a foundation from which to start. You must grow up personally and spiritually in Christ and learn more than what you were taught as a child. This goes back to having a personal relationship with God.

"For at least part of what is meant by saying that Jesus is the truth is that, by virtue of his unique relationship with the Father, he reveals the Father, that is, he makes the Father known. In providing knowledge Jesus provides true beliefs, and if we take that content to be given by a sentence, it seems that Jesus' being the truth is dependent on sentence truth." (Scott, 2005)

We have to live a life that makes our testimonies as to the realities of God's existence to be truth. Our experiences will become our knowledge base that we can share with others. This is why a personal relationship with God is so important. "True belief is necessary for knowledge, and it seems evident that a relationship with Jesus, such as worshipping him, requires certain minimal knowledge of him." (Scott, 2005)

Neil Sinclair said, "Thus, one consequence of my response to the moral belief problem is that evolutionary issues are relevant but not decisive for the issue of the cognitive status of moral convictions." (Sinclair, 2006) This simply meant that we can acknowledge physical facts of what science is trying to observe and record and still believe in the truth not easily seen.

We can change the negative facts in some folks' lives and let them realize there is hope. There are some things about hope that are important:

1. Our hope is based on fact there are people who want to do good for others. You can be one of those persons. God will sometimes have you do for others what they'd never expected. This can also apply to others that God will send to be a blessing to you when you least expected it.

2. God can prepare us for situations that can destroy our hope. The devil will often throw things at you that you thought you couldn't handle. Keeping faith in God will enable you

to handle anything in life that comes your way.

3. The hope and promise in God will get us through life's problems. Sometimes life is fraught with problems that we must go through. We often pray that the problems go away. It is sometimes better to pray for the strength to endure.

Don't let your life problems make you restless and lose faith in God. Even through your problems that made you restless, the Bible said there is hope for the restless.

> **Psalms 10:17 - 18 (NLT)**
> [17] LORD, you know the hopes of the helpless. Surely you will hear their cries and comfort them. [18] You will bring justice to the orphans and the oppressed, so mere people can no longer terrify them.

Fighting through life's problems can sometimes lead us to feel dead inside. The road we travel can seem that we have reached a dead end. Christ can transform dead ends into doorways of hope. Never give up on your walk with Christ! You will know God regardless of your situation when you mature spiritually. Regardless of why you are going through a certain problem look for the opportunity for growth! There is a lesson in every struggle. Sometimes it could be for you to better understand what others are going through or experience. How can you fully understand someone who is having problems paying bills if you have never experienced it yourself to some degree? Having faith and experience in how God works can give you comfort while going through problems.

Comfort in life's problem can come with spiritual maturity. Spiritual maturity does not come easily. We must realize that God is bigger than any problem we face. We must realize that God has expectations of us. What is God's highest expectation of us? I think it is to be like Jesus and to have faith only in Him. The book of Romans tells us we should be more like Christ.

> **Romans 8:28 - 30 (NLT)** [28]And we know that God causes everything to work together for the good of those who love God and are called according to his purpose for them. [29]For God knew his people in advance, and he chose them to become like his Son, so that his Son would be the firstborn among many brothers and sisters. [30]And having chosen them, he called them to come to

> him. And having called them, he
> gave them right standing with
> himself. And having given them
> right standing, he gave them his
> glory.

Believe it or not being like Christ will give us the
courage to face things in ways we never thought
possible. I was able to face debtors with faith enough
to tell them that one day I would pay them off. This
declaration was made through my faith in God even
though I did not know where the money would come
from. I eventually paid off the debtors to whom I
made this declaration and drastically reduced other
debt. This same faith will build you up to face the
people on your job who are out to destroy you.
Through faith God will bless you to get past the
people that mistreat you. We must live in our lives
in complete faith.

Faith

Deuteronomy 1:29 - 31 (NLT)
29"But I said to you, 'Don't be shocked or afraid of them! 30The LORD your God is going ahead of you. He will fight for you, just as you saw him do in Egypt. 31And you saw how the LORD your God cared for you all along the way as you traveled through the wilderness, just as a father cares for his child. Now he has brought you to this place.'

As mentioned before, one of God's biggest expectations from us is to have faith in Him! We should always know that God is capable of providing for us. As human beings, it's not unthinkable that we would sometimes question God. There is no sin in questioning God. Where the sin comes in is when you don't believe that God is capable of solving all our problems. No matter what you are going through, you should know that God is with you and He can do all things. We see things in the natural world but God operates in the supernatural! We should pray that God's deliver us to a place that is in His will. Our will is not always God's will.

25

> **Romans 8:31 - 34 (NLT)** [31]What shall we say about such wonderful things as these? If God is for us, who can ever be against us? [32]Since he did not spare even his own Son but gave him up for us all, won't he also give us everything else? [33]Who dares accuse us whom God has chosen for his own? No one—for God himself has given us right standing with himself. [34]Who then will condemn us? No one—for Christ Jesus died for us and was raised to life for us, and he is sitting in the place of honor at God's right hand, pleading for us.

Christians may ask why they are going through a particular problem or having trouble with a certain person. When the scripture asks, who can come against us, it did not mean that no one would come against us or challenge us. What it meant was that no matter who or what comes against us, you will remain victorious against them. You may feel like you are losing the battle but I challenge you to remain steadfast in God, keep the faith, listen to His voice, and you can make it through the storm you're facing.

Just never turn away from the Lord or allow anything to pull you away from Him.

> **Romans 8:35 - 37 (NLT)** [35]Can anything ever separate us from Christ's love? Does it mean he no longer loves us if we have trouble or calamity, or are persecuted, or hungry, or destitute, or in danger, or threatened with death? [36](As the Scriptures say, "For your sake we are killed every day; we are being slaughtered like sheep.") [37]No, despite all these things, overwhelming victory is ours through Christ, who loved us.

The truth is, sometimes God will allow us to go through certain problems just to show your enemies how powerful He is and that they can't destroy you. It may be a fact that you are under attack, the truth remains is that God can bring you through it all and make you victorious. This truth goes beyond scientific facts. Phil Ryan said, "The view that truth entails correspondence with the facts, although not false, is not helpful. Our understanding of truth must be able to encompass the truth of normative claims and counterfactuals and of "deeper" truths." (Ryan, 2005)

Psalms 9:9 - 10 (NKJV)
[9] The LORD also will be a refuge

27

> for the oppressed, A refuge in times of trouble. [10] And those who know Your name will put their trust in You; For You, LORD, have not forsaken those who seek You.

When we seek God for shelter, those that choose to be your enemy through fact or deed will not be able to destroy you, no matter how hard they try! If it looks like the enemy is going to will, the truth is God can turn your problems into a blessing! It may not always turn out the way you expected but you will come out a victor!

Ryan said, "There continues to be passionate argument today over whether the Bible is literally true. Many deny the Bible's literal truth yet do not hold that the Bible is false. They are therefore wielding some notion of truth other than literal truth. Thus, the Genesis account of creation is taken to be true in some sense, though it is acknowledged not to correspond to the historical facts." (Ryan, 2005)

More of God's ways will be understood with spiritual maturity. There is a common saying among church communities that says God wants you to come as you are. This is quite true but this does not mean that you should remain as you are! When you come to Christ you are born again! Once you are born into God's family, God expects you to grow up.

Hebrews 5:7 - 14 (NLT) [7]While Jesus was here on earth, he offered prayers and pleadings, with a loud cry and tears, to the one who could rescue him from death. And God heard his prayers because of his deep reverence for God. [8]Even though Jesus was God's Son, he learned obedience from the things he suffered. [9]In this way, God qualified him as a perfect High Priest, and he became the source of eternal salvation for all those who obey him. [10]And God designated him to be a High Priest in the order of Melchizedek. [11]There is much more we would like to say about this, but it is difficult to explain, especially since you are spiritually dull and don't seem to listen. [12]You have been believers so long now that you ought to be teaching others. Instead, you need someone to teach you again the basic things about God's word. You are like babies who need milk and cannot eat solid food. [13]For someone who lives

> on milk is still an infant and
> doesn't know how to do what is
> right. [14]Solid food is for those
> who are mature, who through
> training have the skill to
> recognize the difference between
> right and wrong.

God wants us to mature in the Spirit. We have to grow beyond what we were taught as children and/or what we learn as new Christians. There are two facts I've learned about spiritual maturity:

- It's not automatic. You have to make an effort to learn more, to read more, and to gain more faith.

- Mature believers are called disciples. The more disciplined you are, the more God can use you. This applies to any level of discipleship in which you find yourself.

> **Luke 14:25 - 33 (NLT)** [25]A large crowd was following Jesus. He turned around and said to them, [26]"If you want to be my disciple, you must hate everyone else by comparison—your father and mother, wife and children, brothers and sisters—yes, even

your own life. Otherwise, you cannot be my disciple. [27]And if you do not carry your own cross and follow me, you cannot be my disciple. [28]"But don't begin until you count the cost. For who would begin construction of a building without first calculating the cost to see if there is enough money to finish it? [29]Otherwise, you might complete only the foundation before running out of money, and then everyone would laugh at you. [30]They would say, 'There's the person who started that building and couldn't afford to finish it!' [31]"Or what king would go to war against another king without first sitting down with his counselors to discuss whether his army of 10,000 could defeat the 20,000 soldiers marching against him? [32]And if he can't, he will send a delegation to discuss terms of peace while the enemy is still far away. [33]So you cannot become my disciple without giving up everything you own.

Becoming a disciple of Christ is not always comfortable! The Lord will sometimes allow things to happen in your life to get your attention. He wants you to know the only person you really need to continually count on is Him. You must be willing the take up the cross and bear it. Be prepared to withstand any test that comes your way and be prepared to give your testimony when God delivers you from your problem(s).

Matthew 10:34 - 41 (NLT)
[34]"Don't imagine that I came to bring peace to the earth! I came not to bring peace, but a sword. [35] 'I have come to set a man against his father, a daughter against her mother, and a daughter-in-law against her mother-in-law. [36] Your enemies will be right in your own household!' [37]"If you love your father or mother more than you love me, you are not worthy of being mine; or if you love your son or daughter more than me, you are not worthy of being mine. [38]If you refuse to take up your cross and follow me, you are not worthy of being mine. [39]If you cling to your life, you will lose it; but if you give up your life for me, you will find it. [40]"Anyone who receives you receives me, and anyone who receives me receives the Father

who sent me. [41]If you receive a prophet as one who speaks for God, you will be given the same reward as a prophet. And if you receive righteous people because of their righteousness, you will be given a reward like theirs.

A true mark of a disciple is cross bearing. You make the Lord happy when you are willing to make your life about Him and not about you. You must be willing to give up a large part of yourself to serve the Lord. This should not be considered a sacrifice but you should be willing to give up the "self" that could mislead you. This giving up of ones' self should not be looked upon as a bad or negative thing. You will gain more in the process that you could ever imagine.

Matthew 16:24 - 25 (NLT)
[24]Then Jesus said to his disciples, "If any of you wants to be my follower, you must turn from your selfish ways, take up your cross, and follow me. [25]If you try to hang on to your life, you will lose it. But if you give up your life for my sake, you will save it.

33

Dr. Freddy B. Wilson

This is why it is important to be able to discern the voice of the Lord when He is talking to you. The devil will convince you that you should not surrender all to the Lord. As the old saying goes, the devil is a liar! There are three facts you should know about the devil:

1. His power is limited by God

2. God is aware of what the devil does

3. You don't have to fear the devil

You must fully trust in the Lord. Never waiver in your trust in the Lord and know that He can deliver you through anything. Some problems we face are due to bad decisions and/or choices on our part. Sometimes God will allow you to go through something to see who you will call on or if you would trust Him.

Proverbs 3:5 - 6 (NLT) [5] Trust in the LORD with all your heart; do not depend on your own understanding. [6] Seek his will in all you do, and he will show you which path to take.

Life's problems can cause people to feel helpless or hopeless. These feelings can get our attention and make us realize we are not in control of everything in life. Helplessness or hopelessness is God's way of preparing you for salvation. We must always turn to God to help and guide us in life. We must be willing to give up whatever is hindering us from full servitude to God.

> **Hebrews 13:15 - 16 (NLT)**
> [15]Therefore, let us offer through Jesus a continual sacrifice of praise to God, proclaiming our allegiance to his name. [16]And don't forget to do good and to share with those in need. These are the sacrifices that please God.

When you put your total trust and will in the Lord, He will make a way for you in all your needs. There is no better an example of this than when Jesus calmed the storm when all others around Him were afraid.

You must not be willing to place anything before God. This includes anything in life that you can value more than God. Whatever you place before God becomes your God! This includes your family, your house, your car, your money, your alcohol, your music, your drugs, and other people. I have learned along the way that God not only calms the storms in life, but sometimes he calms his children (us) through the storm. Allow God to take care of us in His way and not always in the way that we think things should happen.

> **Matthew 8:23 - 27 (NLT)**
> ²³Then Jesus got into the boat and started across the lake with his disciples. ²⁴Suddenly, a fierce storm struck the lake, with waves breaking into the boat. But Jesus was sleeping. ²⁵The disciples went and woke him up, shouting, "Lord, save us! We're going to drown!" ²⁶Jesus responded, "Why are you afraid? You have so little faith!" Then he got up and rebuked the wind and waves, and suddenly all was calm. ²⁷The disciples were amazed. "Who is this man?" they asked. "Even the winds and waves obey him!"

There is a song sung by J. Moss named, "Florida". This song speaks of the things we put in front of God. Part of the chorus to the song is, "Let's go to Florida, the corridor of the wicked." One of the verses to the song goes on and says, "I know you think now that I lost my grip, but everyone takes a Florida trip. Yours may not be the same as mine, but when you're talking about sin, there's only one kind. It doesn't matter how paid you are, Florida could be a house or a car. Anything that controls your mind, it could be drugs, sex, lying, or wine". J. Moss was not referring to the physical location of the state of Florida. The state of Florida is known as a vacation destination that some young people visit during college spring breaks, etc. These events are known for the sinful acts involving drugs, alcohol, and sex. However, he was referring to the destination in our lives where we go spiritually, sometimes physically, and commit similar acts. You must not place anything in your life in front of God. Your love for God must be seen!

Mark 12:29 - 31 (NLT) [29]Jesus replied, "The most important commandment is this: 'Listen, O Israel! The LORD our God is the one and only LORD. [30]And you must love the LORD your God with all your heart, all your soul, all your mind, and all your strength.' [31]The second is equally important: 'Love your neighbor as yourself. No other commandment is greater than these."

There is an order that I think your love should flow. You should love God first, you second, and then others. Your love flow priority might be different than mine; however, God should always be first.

Notice I never mentioned 'things'. There is nothing wrong in liking some material things but I think many people get lost in their love and/or quest for things. Getting things should not be your main focus in serving God or in your prayer life.

There are three major factors in life: Faith, Family, and Finance. In dealing with any issue the truth is you must first and foremost have faith in God. God has commanded us to have faith in Him.

> **Mark 11:22 (NLT)** [22]Then Jesus said to the disciples, "Have faith in God.

You must say that God is number one in my life. Say to yourself, "I will always have faith and trust in God". Once this is established you must have faith in yourself. You must believe that you can do the things in life that God wants you to do, no matter how daunting tasks may seem.

> **Mark 11:23 (NLT)** [23]I tell you the truth, you can say to this mountain, 'May you be lifted up

and thrown into the sea,' and it will happen. But you must really believe it will happen and have no doubt in your heart.

I feel that God wants you to be blessed. Your continued trust in Him and your will to obey His commands will indeed find you blessed. Your blessings will often occur without your having to do anything. Many of your blessings might come from others.

You must have faith in others. God will place it in the hearts of others a will to bless you. Blessings don't always have to be financially or materially based. Others could be a blessing just by being available for you when you need them. This could sometimes mean that your family is your blessing. God is the origin of family and family life. In order to have a successful family, God has to be first. You should make a declaration that you and your family will serve the Lord.

This declaration should include your priorities in your finances. God blessed us with the money we use to live our everyday lives. We should be happy to pay our tithes out of this money. God will bless us with more and even enable us to do more with the money that remains after we pay our tithes. As a matter of fact, God can guide you on what we should do with our money. It is alright to consult with a financial advisor, but do not make any move until

God says it is OK. Again this is where a close relationship with God is important.

> **Joshua 24:15 (NLT)** [15]But if you refuse to serve the LORD, then choose today whom you will serve. Would you prefer the gods your ancestors served beyond the Euphrates? Or will it be the gods of the Amorites in whose land you now live? But as for me and my family, we will serve the LORD."

In order to have a successful family there must be order. There are important principles to follow in a family. First and foremost, Christ must be the head.

> **1 Corinthians 11:3 (NLT)** [3]But there is one thing I want you to know: The head of every man is Christ, the head of woman is man, and the head of Christ is God.

Even though the Bible established the man as head of the family, and Christ is above him, everyone is significant in the family. They each play important roles to make the family a success. The woman is just as important as the man in making a successful family. The father and mother in a family must allow others to express their gifts to your family. God can put a message in the children of the family that helps the family grow.

What God can do for you is captured in the book of Psalms.

> **Psalms 20:6 - 8 (NLT)** [6] Now I know that the LORD rescues his anointed king. He will answer him from his holy heaven and rescue him by his great power. [7] Some nations boast of their chariots and horses, but we boast in the name of the LORD our God. [8] Those nations will fall down and collapse, but we will rise up and stand firm.

God will bless you with power beyond what you can see. When fighting with the enemies of God, our weapons are not carnal, but are spiritual. This means that even though we are dealing with problems in the earthly realm, our spiritual power provided by God will help us will the battles we face.

> **Psalms 21:8 - 12 (NLT)** [8] You will capture all your

41

enemies. Your strong right hand will seize all who hate you. [9] You will throw them in a flaming furnace when you appear. The LORD will consume them in his anger; fire will devour them. [10] You will wipe their children from the face of the earth; they will never have descendants. [11] Although they plot against you, their evil schemes will never succeed. [12] For they will turn and run when they see your arrows aimed at them.

You have to get your mind straight! Pray to God that He helps you to clear your mind of impure thoughts, sinful acts, vengeance, greed, lust, and any other thing that keeps you from growing in the Lord. Wrongful acts often start in the mind. Dismiss any thoughts of hopelessness. You should focus on the good things in life you want to do and not the disappointments of the past, self-inflicted doubt, and negativity from persons who have told you what you could not do. Paul A. Hense said, "Your life is a reflection of what your thought processes are. What you think reality is eventually becomes reality because of the actions you take in that mindset." (Hense, 2004)

Having the right mindset must be coupled with faith. When you are on your way to your next goal remember there are sometimes setbacks. These setbacks are sometimes meaningful delays that God allows either to bless you at the appropriate time or there is a lesson to be learned. You must be in your right mind to be ready to receive God's blessings. During your planning and thinking always seek the Lord to keep your mind on the right things. "Thought processes make people succeed or fail. Success or failure here is defined as having what you want out of life, not necessarily money or fame. The primary mover is that little mass of gray matter between your ears. Everything in your life, both good and bad, emanates out of that source. How much money you have, who you are married to, where you live, your relationships with other people, etc., are reflections of the processes going on behind your eyes." (Hense, 2004)

You must seek the truth even on your job or at your business. A friend and I discussed how truth affects the workplace. From the article "Truth seekers (by Dr. Sapp)" we determined that "Leaders must teach and emphasize truthfulness or they will more likely get affirmation from their subordinates rather than truthfulness.

The leader who is insecure will not glean the truth about himself and his organization from these uncomfortable truth events and can dishonor the person seeking to tell the truth. Embraced truth will set us free no matter what package it comes in." My friend believed that this was the kind of organization he worked for.

Sapp said, "They must maintain a value system that honors the person seeking to tell the truth. They must not see truth-telling as disloyal behavior. Failure to do this will produce serious hidden problems within the organizations of the Church and make the truthful person an outcast.

Dishonoring the truth-teller is a characteristic of cults. Cultic behavior, which always includes blindness, will result from an overemphasis of loyalty above the truth. Leaders must understand that their own desire for loyalty may overcome truthfulness in their subordinates."

I tried to explain this to my pastor of a church in which I was once active. He seemed receptive at first to my input to mistakes he and other leaders at the church were making but I can tell his attitude changed. He appointed persons to positions only because they appeared loyal and gave money regularly. I could not continue in such dysfunction. True to Dr. Sapp's words, they are having problems keeping people now. I am not glorifying the problems this particular church experienced but sometimes you have to face the fact in order to change the truth about situations.

Truth can vary within our minds. The challenge is figuring out the origins of the information and what it means to us. God can put things in our minds to do but it is up to us to do what he places in our mind to do. Keep in mind, God will never have you do anything that is against His Word as indicated in the bible! There are also things the devil will put in our minds to do that will ultimately destroy us or keep us from reaching an intended destiny. We have to have a personal relationship with God to know the difference in voices. Sometimes our own thoughts can interfere with what God wants us to do. We have to discern our own desires and thoughts from those God places in us.

To be a true believer, you truly have to let go, and let God. There is a series of things going on in your life that you don't understand. Just trust God and ask him the meaning of what you are going through and how you should respond to them. God is Glorious! He has ways of putting you where you need to be and you won't know why. God will put people and things in your life to help guide you in the direction you need to go. Just when you think things are impossible, God is working a way for you! God showed me that I needed to complete this book about his truth and I became determined to finish it. Too many people are looking at just the facts, and not paying attention to God's truth. The truth is God is capable of doing anything. God wants to show out in your life and show others that he is capable! His plan for you and what you need to do is not always about you!

As usual, we may not always understand the purpose of what God places in our minds to do. Sometimes it is very clear what God is telling us. At other times, the message may not be so clear. While God may be leading us to do one thing, other tempting matters will come up to distract us or confuse us. An example is that while I ran into some financial difficulties paying some bills while paying on a few different car loans, I felt it necessary to get rid of two of my vehicles (both were blessings but one more so than the other) for a more fuel-efficient vehicle. I was upside down on the balance of my commuter vehicle but if the loan I requested was approved, it would have saved me a lot of money in monthly payments as well as in the long term.

While I was working two different deals, there were problems that slowed me down and I didn't know why. On 25 Jan 2011, President Barack Obama spoke in the State of the Union address. His speech reminded me that I ultimately wanted to get another business vehicle that would assist me in growing my part-time business. Past lack of successes had me wondering if I should do this and my wife also was against my purchasing the truck. The fact is I had to do something to get back on financial track; the truth is that if I follow the Word of God, He would bless me no matter how impossible the situation looks.

I believed that God had a specific vehicle for me that was actually better than the one I had looked for. I also believed He would make a way for me to get the vehicle despite the fact that I owe a lot more on the vehicle than it is worth. I will have to act on what God leads me to do regardless of what others are telling me. I must also realize that if God wants me to have a new vehicle, it might not be the ones of which I've been primarily looking. God later shows me where I would be better off getting a good vehicle for my teenage daughter to drive. Even though I didn't think I would qualify, he blessed us with a very nice Honda with low miles that looked brand new. When God puts a thought to our minds we sometimes limit what it means or place it on the wrong item, matter, or person.

This puts in mind what happened to me in Virginia in 2006 when I was contemplating buying a newer Toyota Prius or a Camry Hybrid to replace my 2004 Prius. I bought a gold colored Prius at a time that I really wanted a red one. A local dealership had a beautiful new red 2006 Prius on the lot and I got the feeling that I should buy it. After much prayer, driving, and looking at the Prius, God finally answered my prayer and told me not to worry about this Prius for He had something better for me. My response to God was – Hunh! I didn't know what God meant by that.

One day at a later time as I was leaving bible study at a local church I decided to go by another Toyota dealership to look at a Camry Hybrid. I found a selection but I still did not get the feeling that any of these cars were what the Lord was showing me. As I departed there and headed for home, the Lord led me to go by the local Lexus dealership. I just happen to see a beautiful red 2007 Lexus ES 350 that floored me! I thought this would be a wonderful gift to my wife! I called a salesman I knew the next day. He informed that that the vehicle was usually a special-order only color that it had arrived the night I saw it. The only reason they had it was someone ordered it at another dealership and decided to get a different one after it arrived. The dealership I visited traded one of their vehicles for this one at another dealership's customer request. My salesman warned me that that vehicle would go fast! I visited the dealership after I got off work that day. Sure enough, there were other people in the dealership looking at purchasing the vehicle. As I walked out to look at the red Lexus I passed by a beautiful, silver 2007 Lexus GS 450h Hybrid vehicle that I'd never seen before. I was flabbergasted! I asked the salesman if I could drive the vehicle after looking at the other Lexus for my wife. I was really impressed with the comfort and power of the vehicle.

My problem now was that I went there to buy my wife a car and now here I was contemplating buying a vehicle that was priced nearly $20,000 higher than what I would have paid for my wife's. I went away praying what to do! It really bothered me that I would have such a dilemma. After much prayer and debate with myself, I decided to buy the silver car for me. I wondered if I would be approved to purchase such an expensive car. God told me not to worry and He worked it all out. I bought the car on a Friday. Early the next Sunday morning, I woke up about 3:00 am. I felt strongly the Lord telling me to go back and buy the other Lexus for my wife. This really bothered me and I had to wait until Monday to see if the car was still available. When I went into the dealership to try to make another deal, someone else came to my salesman to ask for the keys to test drive the car. I grabbed the keys and told him "no" for this vehicle was sold! That was bold of me for I hadn't been approved to buy it at that time. God blessed me again to buy the second car for my wife.

I wondered how I would be able to afford them. It had been 5 years since that purchase when I wrote these words and we still owned the vehicles. It has taken many miracles along the way to keep them for my wife and I created other debt along the way that made things difficult. God blessed us to pay them off. We now have the titles to both cars. God is so good!

The fact about this situation is that I did not have the credit to make such a purchase but the truth was that God created a way! Some financial experts may say that I should not have incurred such a debt. I say that if you don't do what God will have you do, you could have a lot more to lose! What God will have you do is not always about you! God could be showing someone else what He could do for the faithful. He could also be building you up to be a testimony for someone else. Scientists or philosophers may not want to believe my achievements to be blessings because they cannot repeat them. God is the master of impossibilities for what was once considered impossible.

We sometimes get lost in our own messes. So much so that we get distracted from the things the Lord has for us to do. The truth is God has a plan for every one of his children. The fact is that we are either not listening or are allowing something or someone else to distract us from what we should be doing. These distractors could be living in our home or are at our places of work.

I have experienced this very fact when writing this book. If there was not something distracting me, then it was someone! That someone could be wanting attention from you just because of jealousy that you would have something to pay attention to other than them. Then again, that person could just be a "needy" personality that will try to pull more and more attention from you because that is how they survive – needing attention from someone else to justify their existence.

The difference between fact and truth is that fact is what you are going through. Truth is what God is capable of doing on your behalf. God can take the blemished facts in our lives and apply his truths to turn the facts to glorious achievements!

> **Acts 2:22 - 24 (NKJV)** [22]"Men of Israel, hear these words: Jesus of Nazareth, a Man attested by God to you by miracles, wonders, and signs which God did through Him in your midst, as you yourselves also know— [23]Him, being delivered by the determined purpose and foreknowledge of God, you have taken by lawless hands, have crucified, and put to death; [24]whom God raised up, having loosed the pains of death, because it was not possible that He should be held by it.

As Jesus was being persecuted, his persecutors asked him that if he was the son of God, why he had not delivered himself from their bonds. In response, Jesus only prayed for them and asked the Lord to forgive them for what they were doing to him. Jesus knew he had to pay the price for humanity and only prayed that God will do His will. In the end Jesus's return from the tomb was more miraculous that if he had removed himself from the cross. I feel that Jesus was showing us that we should allow God to fight our battles.

Romans 4:16 - 22 (NKJV) [16] Therefore it is of faith that it might be according to grace, so that the promise might be sure to all the seed, not only to those who are of the law, but also to those who are of the faith of Abraham, who is the father of us all [17] (as it is written, "I have made you a father of many nations") in the presence of Him whom he believed—God, who gives life to the dead and calls those things which do not exist as though they did; [18]who, contrary to hope, in hope believed, so that he became the father of many nations, according to what was spoken, "So shall your descendants be." [19]And not being weak in faith, he did not consider his own body, already dead (since he was about a hundred years old), and the deadness of Sarah's womb. [20]He did not waver at the promise of God through unbelief, but was strengthened in faith, giving glory to God, [21]and being fully convinced that what He had promised He was also able to perform. [22]And therefore "it was accounted to him for righteousness."

Sometimes we have to be reminded why we are here as we serve God. I have seen a lot of embattled ministers in the news lately as well as recently learning of some personal problems being experienced by a pastor I know. On the first hand we all must realize that as Christians, the devil we attack the very foundation that we try to build in our lives. When start allowing ourselves to think our ministries or daily walk is about us or our personal accomplishments, we are prone to failure or severe disappointments!

We must continue to try to be like Christ while living our lives on earth and apply Godly principles to every aspect of our lives. When we pray, we must stop telling God how to go about blessing us. God is capable of blessing us way beyond the way we ask in our prayers. Try not to always understand how God goes about blessing us. We may not understand what is going on as it occurs. People around you that knew your circumstances will be amazed at the things you are able to do in your life without the apparent support systems and methods that people recognize.

> **Mark 2:8 - 12 (NKJV)** [8]But immediately, when Jesus perceived in His spirit that they reasoned thus within themselves, He said to them, "Why do you reason about these things in your hearts? [9]Which is easier, to say to the paralytic, 'Your sins are forgiven you,' or to say, 'Arise, take up your bed and walk'? [10]But that you may know that the Son of Man has power on earth to forgive sins"—He said to the paralytic, [11]"I say to you, arise, take up your bed, and go to your house." [12]Immediately he arose, took up the bed, and went out in the presence of them all, so that all were amazed and glorified God, saying, "We never saw anything like this!"

Regardless of your situation, it has purpose. You may ask yourself how you ended up in the situation or how you got back into a situation after you'd gotten out of it before and now back in it again. Repeating the same situation is common especially in financial situations. We get out of one bit of debt and find ourselves in debt again. These situations may be either God showing you to count on Him only or His keeping you from getting into a worse situation in other matters if you had the money or credit to do a certain thing. For example, your credit score may have kept you from getting a certain car at which you were looking. Your denial of credit may have been God blessing you to not get that particular car for God knew there were problems with it or God had something better for you at a later time or date.

> **Mark 11:22 - 23 (NLT)** [22]Then Jesus said to the disciples, "Have faith in God. [23]I tell you the truth, you can say to this mountain, 'May you be lifted up and thrown into the sea,' and it will happen. But you must really believe it will happen and have no doubt in your heart.

Keep in mind that when you pray, ask God to give you the desires of your heart but only if it was God's will that you have it and that the "it" won't cause you problems. Sometimes we want things that aren't necessarily beneficial to us in the long run. God wants to bless us even if the blessing is just His way of showing others that His children are blessed. Always keep God in mind in whatever you do or desiring to do. We must be careful that the material things God blesses us with doesn't become our God or our primary focus at any given time. Never be selfish with the things God bless you with. Jesus

55

died on the cross for you. It would be a sad day or time when you sacrifice your spiritual relationship with God for the sake of a material thing. That material thing could become a problem or an irritant in your life. Always pray that you can stay in God's will.

> **Acts 2:23 (NLT)** But God knew what would happen, and his prearranged plan was carried out when Jesus was betrayed. With the help of lawless Gentiles, you nailed him to a cross and killed him.

Sometimes God will bless you simply to show others how powerful and blessed believers are. Your blessings are not always about you. Others witnessing your blessing may just inspire them to want to be like you or seek your advice on matters important to them in their lives.

> **Acts 2:23 (NLT)** But God knew what would happen, and his prearranged plan was carried out when Jesus was betrayed. With the help of lawless Gentiles, you nailed him to a cross and killed him.

That problem you face at work or in your family may have been allowed by God. God knows people will come against His children. There is a biblical passage that indicates Jesus told his disciples that just as the enemy will persecute Jesus, they would also persecute his followers. You should boldly face your problems and know that God is aware of what you are facing. Don't take it so personally that people will attack you as a child of God. The devil is attacking and wants you to lose your joy and your faith in the Lord.

> **Romans 4:17 (NLT)** That is what the Scriptures mean when God told him, "I have made you the father of many nations." This happened because Abraham believed in the God who brings the dead back to life and who creates new things out of nothing.

God puts life into what appeared to have been dead. God will put life into possibilities in your life that you once thought were dead. That relationship that you thought was dead can have new life (if that relationship was in God's Will). We should not ask God to give life to something to which we should have never been involved.

This is the kind of life that only God could bring. This could be a new level of living you once thought was not possible for you. God can qualify you for a job you once thought you were not qualified for.

Don't be afraid of the progress in your life that you didn't think could happen to you. I have a friend once turn down a promotion she was offered because she thought she was not qualified for it. When God moves in your life, be prepared to step into a new reality! And don't worry about the people around you who will talk badly about your progress. Keep your concerns on what God expects of you and not on expectations of people.

> **Romans 4:20-25 (NLT)** [20] Abraham never wavered in believing God's promise. In fact, his faith grew stronger, and in this he brought glory to God. [21]He was fully convinced that God is able to do whatever he promises. [22]And because of Abraham's faith, God counted him as righteous. [23]And when God counted him as righteous, it wasn't just for Abraham's benefit. It was recorded [24]for our benefit, too, assuring us that God will also count us as righteous if we believe in him, the one who

raised Jesus our Lord from the dead. [25]He was handed over to die because of our sins, and he was raised to life to make us right with God.

Dealing with the Facts

As Christians, we don't have to deny the existence of problematic facts in our lives. Acknowledging a fact does not mean we accept the fact as something that can't change. We can acknowledge that we are weak, but the truth is God can give us strength to endure. We can acknowledge the fact that we are in debt, but still have the peace of mind to know God will deliver us from our problems. Not all problems are meant to destroy or kill us. God will sometimes allow things to happen to us to see how we respond and see if we turn to Him or turn to something worldly. God does not like for us to depend on anyone or anything above Him. We should not put our sole trust in our friends, family, jobs, or money. God will bless us with and in all these things but we have to put Him first.

I have heard some pastors over the years tell people to not acknowledge a particular problem. I agree that you should not claim a particular diagnosis but you should not deny that the doctors saw a certain problem. To deny what was there is ignorant but we don't have to accept it as it was. God has to power to heal any illness or condition. God may want to heal you through working through doctors. He can work through the doctors to medicate you or operate to remove or fix the problem. God can even perform a miracle that when the doctors look again, the problem they saw would then be gone!

Where the faithful gains strength is through putting our lives and problems in God's hands! He will take care of your problems or show you steps to take to work through them. God may be waiting on you to make a move in a direction He placed in your heart. Through a personal relationship you will know when God is speaking to you. God will never place evil plans or intentions in you. We must be faithful enough to do God's will. Don't be afraid when He tells you to do something positive that you once thought were beyond your capabilities.

God wants us to show Him our faith. Sometimes we say that the devil is attacking us when it could be God allowing things to happen to you so that you can grow and develop. The fact of the problems you face are apparent; the truth is God can take your problems and make them a source of strength to you and encouragement to others. You should never deny that there is a problem; however, you should have the faith in God to know He can make things better, no matter how bad things look.

Don't be afraid of having to go through a problem! You can't always run from problems. It's better to go through a problem and get to the end than to get stuck in the problem. With some people you will hear them complain about a problem for years. Some of them refer to the problem(s) as their "situation". You have to be faithful that God will bless you to move from your situation and on to His blessings. Take the focus off what you see in front of you and move towards the blessings that only faith in God can bring.

A good example of this was when Pharaoh realized he made a mistake in allowing the Israelites to escape. Pharaoh gathered his best chariots and soldiers. Little did Pharaoh know, God already knew what Pharaoh was going to do. The Egyptians began to pursue the Israelites.

> **Exodus 14:10 - 14 (NLT)** [10]As Pharaoh approached, the people of Israel looked up and panicked when they saw the Egyptians overtaking them. They cried out to the LORD, [11]and they said to Moses, "Why did you bring us out here to die in the wilderness? Weren't there enough graves for us in Egypt? What have you done to us? Why did you make us leave Egypt? [12]Didn't we tell you this would happen while we were still in Egypt? We said, 'Leave us alone! Let us be slaves to the Egyptians. It's better to be a slave in Egypt than a corpse in the wilderness!'" [13]But Moses told the people, "Don't be afraid. Just stand still and watch the LORD rescue you today. The Egyptians you see today will never be seen again. [14]The

LORD himself will fight for you.
Just stay calm."

Even when things look their worst, you have to continue to trust God. God and his angels will protect you even if you don't see His hand protecting and guiding you. And as I have said before, God's timing is not our timing. Just because what was asked for has not occurred yet, it does not mean that it won't happen. God might just be preparing us for a much larger testimony than we anticipated! God knows what He is doing so we must learn to trust in this truth.

There are examples in the bible where God was blessing His people and the people began to doubt God. We have to pay attention to the directions in life that God gives us. God knows of our problems even before we are aware of them.

> **Exodus 14:19 (NLT)** [19] Then the angel of God, who had been leading the people of Israel, moved to the rear of the camp. The pillar of cloud also moved from the front and stood behind them.

We don't have to see with our eyes what God is doing in our lives and in whatever circumstance you find yourself. If you have a close relationship with God and you hear Him tell you something to do, you should not be afraid and do what the Lord will have you do, even if it didn't make sense to you initially. I've had many occasions when God told me to do something that I thought was impossible. Every time I did what God told me to do, success followed! God once told me to go back to a bank for a loan I needed. I told God that bank had recently turned me down for that loan (God already knew that). Though apprehensive, I did what God told me to do and went back to the same bank. The bank approved my loan! As I've said in the past, God is the master of possibilities!

Exodus 14:26 - 28 (NLT) [26] When all the Israelites had reached the other side, the LORD said to Moses, "Raise your hand over the sea again. Then the waters will rush back and cover the Egyptians and their chariots and charioteers." [27] So as the sun began to rise, Moses raised his hand over the sea, and the water rushed back into its usual place. The Egyptians tried to escape, but the LORD swept them into the sea. [28]Then the waters returned and covered all the chariots and charioteers— the entire army of Pharaoh. Of all the

Egyptians who had chased the Israelites into the sea, not a single one survived.

You can acknowledge the facts of what you're dealing with, but you should more so state the truth of what God can do. One perspective of a believer is that God is in front of you providing a safe pathway while protecting you from the back. I learned from my current pastor that you must be able to realize to yourself that, "My purpose and progress is a process".

Isaiah 40:28 - 29 (NLT) [28] Have you never heard? Have you never understood? The LORD is the everlasting God, the Creator of all the earth. He never grows weak or weary. No one can measure the depths of his understanding. [29] He gives power to the weak and strength to the powerless.

Conclusion

Our success is already in God's plan. We must learn to discern the voice of God and allow Him to guide us. There are many distractions that will pull us from God's purpose in our lives. Some of the problems we are experiencing are there just to prepare us for our future. They occur either to make us stronger or to facilitate a testimony we can share with others to give them hope. God enables us to do things beyond our normal reach or known capabilities.

The fact is that we sometimes get confused as to exactly what God is leading us to do. That's OK so long as we are willing to stay in the Will of God. The truth is God is guiding us to a wonderful destiny!

References

Burnham, T. L. (March 19, 2003). The Meaning of Truth. *Week Three Comments, DOC702,* 1, Phoenix, University of Phoenix

Craig, H. K. (2006, August). The difference between the truth and the facts. *Contractor*, p. 52.

Gorsuch, R. L. (2002). The Pyramids of Sciences and of Humanities: Implications for the Search for Religious "Truth". *American Behavioral Scientist*, *45*, 1822-1838.

Hense, P. A. (2004, June 1). Truth Is In The Eye Of The Beholder. *Grand Rapids Business Journal*, p. 20.

Holy Bible, New Living Translation, Second Edition, Electronic Edition STEP Files Copyright © 2005, QuickVerse.

McGrath, M. (2005). Lynch on the Value of Truth. *Philosophical Books*, 302-310.

Ryan, P. (2005). Meckler and Baillie on Truth and Objectivity. *JOURNAL OF MANAGEMENT INQUIRY, 14* (No. 2), 120-126.

Scott, M. (2005). The Truth Conditions of Christian Belief: A Critique of Bruce Marshall. *The Journal of Religion*, 43-57.

Dr. Freddy B. Wilson

Sinclair, N. (2006, June). The Moral Belief Problem. *The Author, Journal Compilation*, 249-260.